The Girl on the Train

*A Novel by
Paula Hawkins*

Honest Reviews

© 2015

©Copyright 2015

Disclaimer

Contents

Summary

Opening Segment:

An unknown narrator tells us that "she" is buried near the train tracks, where she can rest without disturbance.

Opening Segment 2:

The narrator tastes blood. They see a silhouette against the light, and hear a voice telling them they made the speaker do it.

Rachel:

July 5, 2013

Every day, Rachel rides the train between Ashbury and London, watching the houses go by.

On the evening train, she is drinking gin and tonic from a can and thinking about the first vacation she took with Tom. She thinks about what she would have done before when the weather was nice on the weekend and how she has no one to enjoy the weather with now.

July 8, 2013

There is a signal where the train almost always stops, and she can see house number fifteen, which is her favorite house to watch. It's an old Victorian, with a fenced garden, and she's seen it so often she has it memorized.

Rachel thinks of the people who live in the house as Jason and Jess. She watches them because she likes how good they look together – Jess small and blonde, and Jason dark-haired and strong. When they aren't outside, she imagines what they might be doing.

In the evening Rachel keeps her back to the other people on the train so they won't see her opening a small bottle of wine. The train passes number fifteen, going too fast for Rachel to see Jason and Jess, and she imagines them again, out on the terrace together. She tries to remember how long it's been since anyone touched her affectionately.

July 9, 2013

When the train stops, Rachel can see Jess out on the patio and tries to keep watching her as the train starts moving again so that she doesn't have to see number twenty-three.

Number twenty-three is the house she lived in for five years. She doesn't want to look, but she always does anyway. She remembers how it hurt to see a pink blind put in place of the white one that used to be in the upstairs window, and how she felt when she saw Anna pregnant. Rachel closes her eyes so she doesn't look at the house.

The evening train is slightly slower than the morning train, but Rachel doesn't mind because she doesn't really want to go back to Ashbury, where she's renting a room from a woman she knew in college. She only intended to stay for a short while, but she's been renting from Cathy for two years, and she feels like she's lost control.

July 10, 2013

In Rachel's mind, Jason is a doctor and he's always flying out to other countries to help after disasters. Jess she imagines working in fashion or music, and having a room upstairs where she paints.

Rachel admits to herself that she doesn't know what Jason and Jess do, or what they look like close, or even what their names are. She only knows them from watching them on the train. She thinks they must be happy and in love, though, like she and Tom were five years ago.

July 11, 2013

When she got home, Rachel drank two bottles of wine and called Tom four times. She doesn't remember what she said. She sees Jess out on the patio and thinks that she looks unhappy. As they pass number twenty-three, Rachel remembers that she left Tom a message saying she loved him and needed to talk to him. She feels ashamed, but tells herself that she's done worse things.

All day, Rachel can't stop thinking about Jess and wondering what she felt was wrong. She thinks Jess looked lonely and that maybe Jason is away on business. She receives a call from Tom, who tells her she has to stop calling because it upsets Anna and advises her to go to AA.

Megan

May 16, 2012

Megan, out on the terrace of number fifteen, hears the train coming and thinks about all the places she could be. She thinks about being back in Holkham by the sea and how it's strange that she misses it.

In the evening she sits out on the terrace and waits for Scott to come home so she can ask him to go out to dinner. She hasn't gotten applications in for classes she wants to take because she was distracted by a woman screaming. She looks out into the garden of another house and sees two women and a baby. The woman with the baby runs into the house, and the other woman stumbles around the garden. Megan goes back inside and thinks about how she misses the gallery she owned and how no one would recognize her settled down and married. She tells herself she'll get a job at the end of the summer.

August 14, 2012

Megan gets ready to go take care of a baby for the people down the lane. She misses the gallery and the clothes she used to wear. Scott is happy she decided to do it because he thinks it will make her want children, but she hates it, and she thinks that Anna is jumpy and too wrapped up with the baby to be interesting.

August 16, 2012

Megan quits her job as a nanny. She thinks of all the different people she's been, and how she can reinvent herself again.

September 20, 2012

Megan can't sleep; she thinks about how she was supposed to go on a road trip with her brother Ben before he was killed in a motorbike accident. She decides to go to a therapist. Dr. Kamal Abdic is reassuring and attractive. Megan tells him she has panic attacks and insomnia. She imagines him touching her.

September 25, 2012

In the evening, Scott is home late and Megan goes out for a walk. An unnamed man who is obviously familiar drives by in his car and smiles at her.

Rachel

July 12, 2013

Rachel sees Jess kissing a man who isn't Jason in their garden, and remembers the way it felt to find out Tom was having an affair. She is furious with Jess.

July 13, 2013

Rachel drinks at a pub and decides to go see Jason.

July 14, 2013

Sunday morning, Rachel wakes with no memory of the night before and a bad lump on her head. She has a call waiting from Tom, who says she scared Anna and he spent most of the night driving around looking for her.

Megan

October 2, 2012

Megan can't sleep and calls a man, hanging up when he gets angry. She tells her therapist that Scott checks up on her all the time.

October 13, 2012

Megan asks an acquaintance named Tara to cover for her while she meets a man at a hotel. He tells her it can't happen again, but she knows it will.

Rachel

July 15, 2013

Cathy gives Rachel eviction papers with four weeks to find a new place. Rachel wonders where she went wrong, and thinks it must have been when she decided she needed a baby. She discovers that Megan Hipwell, the woman she called Jess, has missing since the night she went to see Jason.

Megan

January 10, 2013

Megan tells Kamal about Mac, the man she met when she was seventeen and lived with for two years near Holkum. She tells him Mac broke her heart when he left.

February 8, 2013

Kamal asks Megan if she is afraid of her husband, and she tells him she isn't. When she tries to kiss him, he tells her no.

Rachel

July 16, 2013

Rachel goes to Witney to see if being there will help her remember the night she was blackout drunk. Megan is still missing, and she thinks the police will only look at her husband because they didn't know she had a boyfriend. She writes down her theories about what happened to Megan.

In Whitney, Rachel walks by the underpass and thinks she sees herself there, bleeding. On the train home, she gets a call from Cathy that the police are at the house to speak with her.

July 17, 2013

Rachel tells the police that she didn't speak with Tom on the night Megan disappeared, and lies to them about her job and how drunk she was that night. She decides to go to the station and tell them the truth.

When she tells the police the truth about the night, they point out that she once broke into Tom and Anna's house and took the baby. Rachel denies it. She walks out and sits in a park having lunch, thinking about how not being able to have a child made her depressed and how her drinking made Tom pull away. When she returns to the station, the police ask her about her constant calls to Tom and her refusal to leave him and Anna alone. They suggest that she mistook Megan for Anna while drunk and attacked her. Rachel tells them about the man she saw Megan kissing. As she leaves, they warn her to stay away from Tom and Anna.

July 18, 2013

Rachel emails Scott to tell him she has information about Megan. On the train, she sees a red-haired man she remembers talking to the night she went see Jason, but realizes too late that she could ask him what happened.

Megan

March 7, 2013

Megan discusses leaving with the man she's having an affair with, but when she wakes up in the morning he's gone.

Rachel

July 19, 2013

Rachel hasn't had a drink in three days. She still hasn't heard from Scott. She goes to the station and identifies the man she saw Megan with. That evening, she has gin and tonic to celebrate the police taking her seriously.

July 20, 2013

Rachel wakes and remembers sending an email to Tom. She checks her inbox and finds an answer from Scott to an email she sent while she was drunk that claimed she knew Megan from the gallery. Scott asks to speak in person, and she goes to meet him.

Anna

July 20, 2013

It is Anna's birthday. She thinks of how happy she is with Tom despite Rachel, but that evening she sees Rachel walking down Blenheim Road and Tom finds her pale and shaking.

Rachel

July 21, 2013

Rachel tells Scott about seeing Megan with another man from the window of the train. Scott believes it could be her therapist. The next day, Scott calls her to talk about it, and confesses that he and Megan fought the night she disappeared, and he didn't go after her when she walked out.

July 22, 2013

The papers announce that a suspect has been arrested in Megan's case. She fears it was Scott and gets off at Witney. When she goes to knock on the door, he pulls her into the house.

Megan

March 21, 2013

Megan is angry with her lover, who has stopped calling her. She decides she will call his home if he doesn't answer. She goes to her therapy appointment and tries to kiss Kamal, but he won't allow it. On her way home, she plots revenge.

Rachel

July 22, 2013

Scott warns Rachel that she could have been seen and tells her that the man they arrested is Kamal Abdic. His mother shows

Rachel out. As she leaves, Tom and Anna see her coming out the door.

Anna

July 22, 2013

Anna worries about seeing Rachel, but Tom advises against calling the police.

Rachel

July 23, 2013

Abdic is released due to lack of evidence. Rachel drinks.

July 24, 2013

Rachel remembers calling Scott the night before. She finds two missed calls. When she calls him back, he tells her the police told him she's an unreliable witness and hangs up.

July 26, 2013

Rachel receives a call from Tom and asks him what happened the night she can't remember. He tells her that Anna saw her at the station and he went out to look for her but couldn't find her.

July 29, 2013

Rachel gets off the train at Witney to see if she can find the red-haired man. Instead, she runs into Scott, who takes her back to the house because it's raining. They discuss Anna and Kamal.

August 1, 2013

After days of heavy rain, Megan's body is discovered in Corly Wood, a few miles from Blenheim Road.

Megan

June 13, 2013

Megan goes to Kamal at his home to tell him the rest of her story. She confesses that she had a baby with Mac who drowned when Megan fell asleep with her in the tub. After, Megan kisses Kamal, and he allows it.

Rachel

August 3, 2013

Rachel runs into the red-haired man on the train. She remembers someone trying to hit her, and, afraid, moves to the back of the train where she has a memory of Anna walking away from her in a blue dress.

August 4, 2013

Rachel calls Scott and he tells her that he called her on accident before, but he reluctantly agrees to meet with her. She tells him that she was there the night Megan went missing, and he asks her to try to remember. She makes an appointment with Dr. Abdic. Though she intends to try for information, she finds herself speaking with him about all the troubles in her life. She finds herself relaxing around him, but his smile frightens her.

August 7, 2013

While out for a walk after a nightmare about Tom being angry with her, Rachel sees a tabloid headline about Megan killing her child.

Anna

August 7, 2013

Anna tells Tom they have to move, but he tells her they don't have the money.

Rachel

August 7, 2013

Scott calls Rachel and asks if he can come to her house because his is surrounded by reporters. He tells her that he found out Megan was pregnant when she died. He falls asleep in Rachel's bed.

August 8, 2013

After another visit with Kamal, where he helps her work through not being able to get pregnant, Rachel wonders if she was wrong about him before.

August 9, 2013

Scott asks Rachel to come to his house. They drink, and fall into bed together.

Megan

June 20, 2013

Megan tells Kamal that Mac left the night after the baby died, and never came home. He suggests she try to contact him for closure, and tells her again that they can't sleep together any longer.

Rachel

August 10, 2013

Rachel wakes up in Scott's bed. She begins to feel disgusted by him. When she leaves, she sees Anna, who runs, but watching Anna walk away makes her feel afraid again.

Anna

August 10, 2013

Tom promises to deal with Rachel, but Anna decides the next time she sees her she'll call the police.

Rachel

August 12, 2013

Tom asks Rachel to meet with him in person. He makes her promise not to see Scott again.

August 13, 2013

Rachel dreams about seeing a blue dress by the side of the tracks, and Jason choking Jess. She goes to see Dr. Abdic again, and tells him about attacking Tom with a golf club while she was blackout drunk, but that she doesn't remember being angry. She remembers being afraid.

She goes to Witney after, to see if it will jog her memory, and remembers seeing Tom pulling up near the overpass in his car. She remembers seeing a woman speak to him, then get in.

Anna

August 13, 2013

Anna sees Rachel standing on the road, looking up at the house and calls the police.

August 14, 2013

Anna discovers that Tom met Rachel in person after he told her they'd only spoken on the phone. She remembers him telling her in the early days of their relationship that he was a good liar. She attempts to get into his laptop, but he arrives home before she can crack the password.

Rachel

August 15, 2013

Rachel goes to Scott's home after he asks her to meet him, and he tells her that Megan's child wasn't his or Kamal's. He asks her if she knew about it. When she tries to leave, he locks her in an upstairs bedroom while he goes through her purse, and threatens her before he releases her.

August 16, 2013

Rachel goes to the police to make a report. On the train home, she meets the red-haired man again and he tells her he saw her at the underpass watching her ex-husband and a woman leaving together in a car.

August 17, 2013

Rachel calls Tom to ask him what happened, and he tells her that Anna was home with the baby and to stop calling.

August 18, 2013

As she begins to fall asleep, Rachel remembers Tom standing over her in the underpass and hitting her with his car keys.

Anna

August 17, 2013

Tom walks out on Anna to go to the gym after he finds out she didn't tell him that Rachel left a note in their mailbox. As she's stripping their bed, she finds his gym bag, and inside it she finds a phone with meeting times texted to it.

August 18, 2013

Anna wakes up in the middle of the night and goes downstairs with the phone. There are no messages on the voicemail. It prompts her to change the greeting, and when she does the voice of the current greeting is a woman's voice she recognizes.

Rachel

August 18, 2013

Remembering that Tom hit her, Rachel begins to remember other things, times Tom had told her she behaved differently than she thought. And she remembers that the woman who got into Tom's car that night was not Anna, but Megan. She takes the train down to Blenheim Street, and rings Tom and Anna's doorbell. When Anna doesn't answer the door, Rachel climbs over the fence and finds her in the backyard. She tells Anna that they need to go while Tom is out.

Anna

August 18, 2013

Rachel tells Anna that Tom lies about everything. Anna acknowledges that Tom was having an affair with Megan. Rachel asks her if Megan's baby could have been his, and tells her that she saw Megan getting into Tom's car the night he disappeared. They turn, and find Tom watching them from the kitchen window.

Megan

July 12, 2013

Megan calls Kamal to tell him that she's pregnant. He tells her she won't make the same mistakes with this baby that she did with her daughter.

July 13, 2013

When Megan tells Scott she had an affair, he chokes her and she locks herself in her room, packs a bag and tries to contact the baby's father. When he doesn't answer, she threatens to go to his house. She walks out of her home, telling Scott that if he follows her she'll never come back.

She walks to the park and tries the number again, then turns to walk home. She's passing the overpass when she sees Tom coming out of it, and he tells her they'll drive somewhere. She gets in the car with him, feeling as though she's being watched.

Rachel

August 18, 2013

Tom asks what's going on, and Rachel tells him that he hit her, that he got in the car with Megan. He assures Anna that Rachel is lying. Anna tells him she knows he was having an affair and that she threw the phone over the fence. Tom tells her the truth about him and Megan, that she and Rachel are both weak and that's why he had the affairs. He picks up the baby, and Rachel takes Anna outside to calm her down when she starts screaming. She tells her to distract him while she calls the police.

As Rachel begins to make the call, Tom tackles her and drags her back into the house.

Megan

July 13, 2013

Megan and Tom drive to Corly Wood, where she tells him she's pregnant and that he might be the father. He tells her to get rid of it, and she tells him she'll make him pay. He hits her. He tells her she made him do it.

Rachel

August 18, 2013

Rachel sits with Anna and Tom in their living room. Tom tells them about killing Megan and why he did it. When he goes to the fridge, Rachel tries to run. Tom hits her, drags her back into the kitchen, and tells Anna to go upstairs. When she's gone, he hits Rachel again.

Anna

August 18, 2013

Anna thinks about letting Tom kill Rachel, but she knows that he'll never trust her now that she knows he killed Megan. She goes downstairs and sits with him, and when Rachel begins to wake up she goes into the hall and takes the phone, then sits at the bottom of the stairs and listens.

Rachel

August 18, 2013

Rachel tells Tom he doesn't have to kill her because she still loves him and she won't tell anyone. He tells her she's easy, and kisses her against the counter. She reaches into the drawer behind her, and when she finds what she's looking for she stomps on his foot and knees him in the face, then runs out toward the fence. He comes after her, and she stabs him in the neck with the corkscrew she took from the drawer.

September 10, 2013

After Rachel stabbed Tom, the police came. She and Anna tell them it was self-defense. Stories about Tom come out in the papers, and Rachel finds out that most of what he told her about himself was untrue.

Rachel leaves Ashbury and travels. She visits Holkham, where Megan was buried with her daughter. She sits in her hotel and remembers Anna coming out after her, twisting the corkscrew deeper into Tom's throat. They told the police that Anna tried to save him.

She hopes her nightmares will stop, and goes to sleep so she can get up in the morning to get on the train.

Review

There is little to say about Paula Hawkin's *The Girl on the Train* that isn't positive. Beautifully written, it pulls the reader through the twists of its plot at a breathless pace. That is not to say that it does not have its quiet moments. The genius of Hawkin's work is that it is not only a thriller, not only a murder mystery. Through its shifting point of view, it explores human emotion on a level that most books in its genre cannot reach.

Rachel, the titular girl on the train, is a character reaching the bottom of a downward spiral that began when her ex-husband left her for another woman. She is a drunk, who can't seem to leave her former partner alone. She is also very lonely. It is this loneliness, despite the extremes of her behavior, which makes her so relatable, and so sympathetic. Even before becoming aware of the depth of tragedy in her story, the reader feels for Rachel, caught behind the windows of the train, looking out on other people's lives and imagining them happy because she cannot be. There is a kind of naiveté to the way she looks at the world, believing that Jason and Jess, the imaginary couple she lays over the people who live at number fifteen Blenheim Road, can be perfectly in love, or perfectly anything.

Rachel's Jess, whose true name is Megan, is not happy. She is haunted by her past, and by her inability to settle down with her husband and live the way she believes she should. Like Rachel, she has been touched by tragedy, and has never been able to let it go. Though much of her narration is centered on the set of adulterous affairs that end in her murder, Megan too is relatable, a character the reader can see themself in even when they would not take the same path.

The final point of view character, who speaks only a handful of times, is Anna, the woman Rachel's husband Tom left her for. As a reader, she was the character I connected the least with. She was not hard enough to enjoy hating, too vain and possessed of too little empathy to truly care for. Even she, however, was not relegated only to one role. Just as Rachel becomes more than a lonely drunk, and Megan is not only the victim she initially is placed as, Anna is not only 'the other woman.' She is a woman desperately in love with a man whose lies she doesn't realize until it is too late, and a mother who cares deeply for her child.

These characters, together, tell a story that none of them could fully tell on their own. While some might not appreciate the fairly rapid shifts between points of view, I felt that the nature of the plot made them, if not absolutely necessary, at least very well suited. The narration, which transitions from morning to evening quite quickly through most of the book, was similarly apropos.

There is no padding or wasted space in *The Girl on the Train.* Every line contributes to the plot, and even the smallest details are relevant. In the tradition of the very best mysteries, it is a book that requires a second reading. There is nothing formulaic in Hawkin's plot.

On a first read, the realization of who killed Megan Hipwell is a revelation, telegraphed just enough that as the pieces began to fit together it feels like precisely the place the book was leading all along, if only the reader could have seen it sooner, but not so much that it does not come as a thrilling shock. The second read reveals the little lies that hint at a hidden truth, the second affair that at first seemed to be only one.

One thing I did note while reading, though it is not necessarily a criticism, is that while no one in Hawkin's world is perfect, the men in particular seem to be hiding a dark side. Tom, who is we initially see only through Rachel's rose-colored glasses is not only a cheater, but a compulsive liar, an abuser, and a murderer. Rachel's blackout drinking kept her from remembering, but as she begins to regain those moments, the reader is chilled as much as she is by the fear she feels without knowing why.

Scott, whom Rachel imagined as protective and gentle, is possessive. He goes through Megan's emails and checks her phone. During her sessions with the therapist, Dr. Abdic asks her if she is afraid of him, and warns her that his behavior is emotional abuse. She brushes it off, but when she tells Scott of the affair she was having the abuse escalates to physical. Later, he locks Rachel in a room and tells her as he lets her go that he should have snapped her neck.

Even Damien, Cathy's boyfriend who only shows up a few times in the book and is mostly just mentioned, seems to be less than savory. The only man who does not turn out to be dangerous is the red-haired man who walked with Rachel for a time on the night she went to Blenheim Road, and he seems to be as much a drunk as she is.

Overall, *The Girl on the Train* is a read well worth the time. The mystery, the need to know what happened on the night Rachel can't remember, the night Megan went missing, makes it hard to set aside even for a moment. Unexpected twists in the plot were frequent enough to keep me guessing, but not so thrown about they began to feel stock. It is a unique book – a thriller with its roots in the heart. It is Rachel's desire for belonging that sets events in motion, and her need for attention that keep them moving forward. The reader wants to know as much as she does what secrets are hiding behind the door of number fifteen Blenheim Road, but that isn't all I wanted. I wanted to see her succeed, to see her find a way to move on from the past that still had her in its clutches, and I found her evolution as a character, moving apace with the evolution of the plot, incredibly satisfying.

11313801R00021

Printed in Great Britain
by Amazon.co.uk, Ltd.,
Marston Gate.